796·334/129305

The F.A. Guide to the Laws of the Game

*A Teaching Programme Devised by
Learning Systems Ltd*

Published on behalf of
The Football Association

HEINEMANN : LONDON

William Heinemann Ltd.
LONDON MELBOURNE TORONTO
CAPE TOWN AUCKLAND

First published 1969

© The Football Association 1969

Printed in Great Britain
Spottiswoode, Ballantyne and Co. Ltd.
London and Colchester

ANSWERS TO POST-TEST ON SECTION 6

1. Goal-kick.
2. Outside the penalty-area and at least 10 yards from the ball.
3. *a.* Re-take the kick.
   b. Caution the players for ungentlemanly conduct.
   c. Indirect free-kick to opposing team.
   d. Allow the goal.
   e. Re-take the kick.
   f. Re-take the kick.
4. No, the match must be ended as soon as the goalkeeper has saved the ball.
5. Yes.

Foreword

It has often been said that much of the charm and popularity of Association Football lies in its simplicity. Basically all that is required to be able to play the Game is a ball and a reasonably level piece of ground, but obviously all games benefit when played in accordance with Laws which are universally acceptable and applicable.

In this respect Association Football is singularly blessed. There are but seventeen Laws which are readily and quickly assimilated by every player from an early age. Nevertheless, the wisest of us are never too old to learn and a 'Teaching Manual' of this kind will, I am sure, provide a useful appendix to the Laws of the Game.

'Programming' is now accepted as a modern method of teaching. It is encouraging to know that experiments carried out some two years ago by the Royal Naval Football Association Referee Recruits, provided results well above those achieved previously by traditional methods.

Much of the value of the book will be lost, however, if the young referee or player does not acquaint himself with the Laws as authorized by the International Football Association Board. The Laws are published in the F.A. *Referee's Chart and Player's Guide to the Laws of the Game* and a copy of this booklet may be obtained from the Football Association, price 1*s.* 9*d.,* including postage.

To all those about to begin active participation in the Game as a referee or a player, I recommend this book. Football is a recreation to enjoy. It becomes so much more enjoyable when played fairly in accordance with the Laws.

Chairman,
The Football Association,
22 Lancaster Gate,
London, W.2.

POST-TEST ON SECTION 6

1. The ball goes directly into the opposing goal from an indirect free-kick. What is the referee's decision?

2. Where must opposing players stand when a player is taking a free-kick from inside his own penalty-area?

3. What is the referee's decision in these circumstances?

   a. A player takes a free-kick inside his own penalty-area and kicks it to the goalkeeper who picks it up and clears it up field.

   b. As a player takes a free-kick, two opposing players wave their arms and shout 'He will miss it'.

   c. A player takes a penalty-kick. The ball hits the cross-bar and rebounds to the kicker who kicks the ball a second time.

   d. The goalkeeper moves his feet just before a penalty-kick is taken and the ball goes into the goal.

   e. Before the penalty-kick is taken one of the attacking side enters the penalty-area. The ball goes straight into goal.

   f. Players of both sides enter the penalty-area before the ball is in play from a penalty-kick.

4. Play has been extended for a penalty-kick to be taken. After the kick the goalkeeper stops the ball which rebounds to an attacker who kicks it into goal. Should the referee allow the goal?

5. Play has been extended for a penalty. The goalkeeper half stops the ball but it rolls past him over the goal-line. Should the referee allow the goal.

Answers on page 241 (bottom).

This programme is intended to teach the Laws of Association Football to potential referees. The programme can also be used by players and football supporters who wish to be instructed in the Laws of the Game. The programme assumes a basic knowledge of how the game is played.

The objectives of the programme are:

1. that a potential referee, after working through the programme in conjunction with the Referee's Chart, should be able to answer the Class III Referee and the County Referee examination papers;
2. that a student should be able to answer questions on the Laws of the Game as explained in the Referee's Chart;
3. that a student should be able to answer questions on the application of the Laws of the Game in given situations arising in the course of play.

The programme has been prepared in consultation with instructors from the Royal Naval Physical Training School, Portsmouth and the programme has been tested on referees, physical training instructors, and seamen from the Physical Training School.

HOW TO WORK THROUGH THE PROGRAMME

Follow the numbers at the top of the page; then return to the beginning of the book and follow the numbers at the bottom of the page. Reverse the book, following page numbers at the top and finally again at the bottom.

Read each page carefully. On most pages you will be asked a question about what you have been reading. You may be asked a direct question, or to select the correct answer from two or three alternatives, or to write in words that have been omitted.

After you have written your answer, turn over and check what you have written with the correct answer given at the top of the next page.

It is quite permissible, if you find it necessary, to glance back at a page you have already seen.

Now turn to page 4 (top).

ANSWERS TO POST-TEST ON SECTION 5

1. *a.* Direct free-kick.
   b. Indirect free-kick.
   c. Indirect free-kick.
   d. Indirect free-kick.
   e. Penalty.
   f. Direct free-kick.
   g. Direct free-kick.
   h. Penalty.
2. *a.* Kicking or attempting to kick an opponent.
   b. Tripping an opponent.
   c. Jumping at an opponent.
   d. Charging an opponent in a violent or a dangerous manner.
   e. Charging an opponent from behind unless he is obstructing.
   f. Striking or attempting to strike an opponent.
   g. Holding an opponent with hand or arm.
   h. Pushing an opponent with hand or arm.
   i. Handling the ball.
3. *a.* Intentionally.
   b. By a defender.
   c. In the penalty-area.
   d. When the ball is in play.
4. *a.* goal-area
   b. is not
   c. obstructing.

Now turn back to page 205 (bottom) for Section 6.

Section 1 The Field of Play, the Goals, the Ball, the Players and their equipment

THE FIELD OF PLAY

The names of the parts of the field of play and the position-ing of the flags are shown in the diagram of the field.

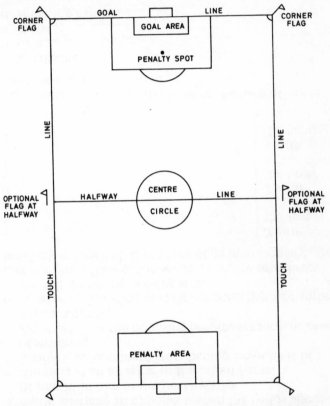

Corner flagposts must be at least 5 feet high and must not be pointed. A quarter circle with a radius of 1 yard is drawn from each corner flag.

Flags at the halfway line are optional. If there are flags at halfway, they must be at least 1 yard *outside the touchline*.

(Go straight on.)

POST-TEST ON SECTION 5

1. State whether the following offences should be penalized by a penalty, an indirect free-kick or a direct free-kick.

    a. Pulling an opponent's shirt.
    b. Goalkeeper carrying the ball more than four steps.
    c. Dangerous play.
    d. Fairly charging an opponent when the ball is about to be passed to him in the penalty-area.
    e. Jumping at an attacker in the penalty-area.
    f. Charging an opponent from behind when he is not obstructing.
    g. An attacker in the opposing penalty-area intentionally trips a defender.
    h. A defender standing outside the penalty-area handles the ball inside the penalty-area.

2. List the nine offences for which a penalty or a direct free-kick is awarded, if they are done intentionally.

    a.
    b.   } *3* with
    c.   the feet
    d.
    e.   } 2 with
    f.   the body
    g.
    h.   } 4 with
    i.   the hands

3. For a penalty to be awarded one of the nine offences must have been committed.

    a. intentionally,
    b. by a_____
    c. in the_____
    d. when the ball is_____

4. It is an offence to charge the goalkeeper

    a. when he is inside his own_____
    b. provided that he (is not/is) holding the ball.
    c. and provided that he is not_____

    Answers on page 239.

When the referee visits the ground before the match, he will check the flagposts.

1. Would he approve of halfway flags on the touchline?

2. Would he approve of corner flags that are 5½ feet high?

3. Are flagposts necessary at the halfway line?

Continued from page 60 (top).

Yes.

....

We have explained that the referee has discretionary power

1. to stop play for any infringement of the laws;

2. to_____ a player for misconduct or ungentlemanly behaviour;

3. to_____ a player for violent conduct or persistent misconduct;

4. to_____ the game because of the weather or serious disorder.

Turn to page 64 (bottom).

ANSWERS TO POST-TEST ON SECTION 4

1. *a.* he is in his own half of the field.
   b. there are at least two opponents nearer to their own goal-line than he is.
   c. the ball last touched an opponent.
   d. the ball is received direct from a goal-kick, a corner-kick, a throw-in or when dropped by the referee.
2. Indirect free-kick.
3. *a.* No, because there were two opponents between B and the goal-line when the ball was passed by A .

   b. Yes, as there were not two opponents between B and the goal-line when A centred.

   c. Yes, as the ball was not received direct from the corner-kick.

   d. No, as B is not interfering with play.

Now turn back to page 151 (top) for Section 5.

---

1. No.
2. The moment that the ball is saved by the goalkeeper.

....

Now turn to Post-Test on Section 6, page 240 (bottom).

1. No.
2. Yes.
3. No.
....

The dimensions of the field of play and its parts are shown on the diagram.

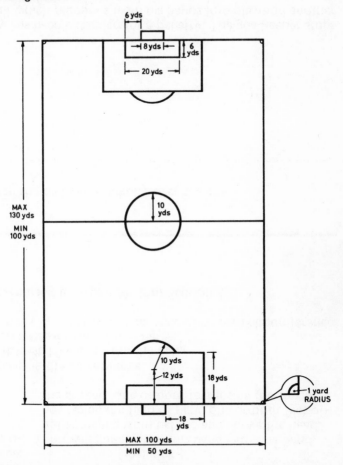

Although you need not try to remember all the dimensions now, note that although maximum and minimum measurements are given for the size of the field of play, the length of the field must always exceed the breadth.

(Go straight on).

ANSWERS TO POST-TEST ON SECTION 3

1. *a.* Re-take the kick.
   b. Indirect free-kick.
2. When the whole of the ball crosses the whole of the line between the goalposts and under the crossbar.
3. *a.* Goal   *c.* Goal
   b. Goal   *d.* Goal-kick
4. Any of: Throwing underarm, throwing with one hand, not throwing from behind and above the head, not facing the field of play, one or both feet off the ground, one or both feet inside the touch-line.
5. *a.* Outside the penalty-area.
   b. At least 10 yards from the ball.
6. When it has left the penalty-area.
7. When it has travelled the distance of its own circumference.

Now turn back to page 124 (top) Section 4.

---

1. Yes
2. When the ball passes wholly over the line.

....

Play has been extended for a penalty. The goalkeeper stops the ball which rebounds from his hands into play and another attacker kicks it into the goal.

     1. Should the goal be allowed?

     2. When will the referee blow his whistle to end the match?

It is the duty of the referee to see that the ground is correctly and clearly marked before the match.

The lines marking the ground should not be more than 5 inches wide and the width of the lines is included in the areas of the field of play.

If the ball is on the touchline itself, will the ball be in play?

2. to caution;
3. to send off;
4. to suspend or terminate.

....

If a player is seriously injured, the referee must stop the play at once. If a player is slightly injured, the game is not to be stopped until the ball goes out of play. When the play has been stopped, seriously injured players must go to or be removed to outside the touchline as soon as possible so that the game can be resumed. Injured players should not be treated on the field of play unless they cannot move or be moved to outside the touchline. A trainer is not allowed on the field to treat a player without the referee's permission.

(Go straight on.)

POST-TEST ON SECTION 4

1. A player is off-side if he is nearer his opponents' goal-line than the ball at the moment that the ball is played, unless . . . give the four exceptions.

2. What is the penalty for being off-side?

3. Look at each of these diagrams and state whether player

   B would be penalized for off-side and give the

   reason for your answer.

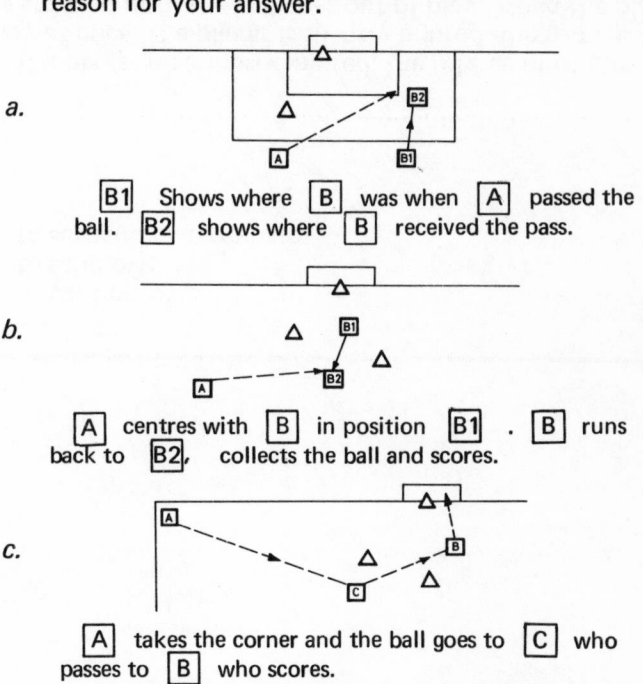

a.

   B1 Shows where B was when A passed the ball. B2 shows where B received the pass.

b.

   A centres with B in position B1 . B runs back to B2, collects the ball and scores.

c.

   A takes the corner and the ball goes to C who passes to B who scores.

d.

   A has come down the left touchline, and centres the ball. B is on the right touchline.

   Answers on page 179 (top).

Yes, as the width of the line is included in the field of play.

....

1. Is the width of the line marking the penalty-area included in the penalty-area?

2. What is the maximum permissible width of the lines marking the field of play?

3. Is it permissible for the field of play to be square?

If the referee notices that a player has been injured and decides that it is serious, should he

    a. stop the game?
    b. wait till the ball goes out of play?

(Select the correct answer)

When will the referee allow the player to be treated on the field of play?

POST-TEST ON SECTION 3

1. What action is taken by the referee

   a. if at the kick-off the kicker kicks the ball into his own half?
   b. if at the kick-off the kicker kicks the ball a second time after it has travelled the distance of its own circumference?

2. When is a goal scored?

3. What is the referee's decision in the following circumstances?

   a. The ball enters the goal direct from a corner-kick.
   b. A defender touches the ball with his hand in an attempt to save a goal but the ball enters the goal.
   c. The ball rebounds from the referee into the goal.
   d. From a throw-in the player throws the ball directly into his opponent's goal.

4. Give three examples of a foul throw.

5. Where must opposing players stand when

   a. a goal-kick is taken?
   b. a corner-kick is taken?

6. When is the ball in play after a goal-kick?

7. When is the ball in play after a corner-kick?

Answers on page 178 (top).

1. Yes.
2. 5 inches.
3. No, the length must exceed the breadth.

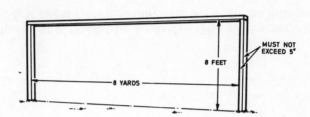

THE GOALS

Note that the two upright posts have to be 8 yards apart and that the measurement is from the inside of the posts.

Note that the lower edge of the horizontal crossbar has to be 8 feet from the ground.

Note that the width of the posts and the crossbar shall not exceed 5 inches.

The goalposts and the crossbar may be square, rectangular, round, half-round, or elliptical in shape.

(Go straight on)

---

a. stop the game.
When he cannot be moved to the touchline.

The referee will normally stop and re-start play by blowing his whistle. However, when he is about to award an indirect free-kick, he will raise his arm as well. The other players then know that an indirect and not a direct free-kick is about to be taken.

Finally, remember that the referee's decision on facts concerned with the play is FINAL. If the referee awards an indirect free-kick and both captains politely tell him that he is wrong, will he change his mind?

2

b. award a direct free-kick.

....

List the nine offences for which a direct free-kick is awarded.

Offences committed with the feet:

1.
2.
3.

Offences committed with the body:

4.
5.

Offences committed with the hands:

6.
7.
8.
9.

Turn back to page 180 (bottom).

_____

Play has been extended for a penalty. The goalkeeper half stops the ball but it rolls past him over the goal-line into goal.

1. Should the referee allow the goal?

2. When will he blow his whistle to end the match?

Turn to page 236 (bottom).

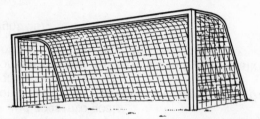

Nets may be attached to the posts, crossbar, and the ground behind the goals provided that they are properly supported and give the goalkeeper plenty of room.

(Go straight on)

No, his decision is final.

....

The referee may change his decision and cancel a goal, which he has allowed, in the following circumstances.

If the game has not been re-started,
If the linesman saw an offence that the referee did not see,
If the offence occurred in the play just before the goal was scored.

An attacking player intentionally stops the ball with his hands before kicking it into the goal. The referee's view of the player was blocked. The referee blows his whistle for a goal. The linesman signals an offence and is consulted by the referee.
Can the referee cancel his decision?

Yes.

....

A goalkeeper can handle the ball in his own penalty-area. Therefore the offence of handling does not apply to the goalkeeper in his own penalty-area.

The goalkeeper falls on the ball and handles it outside his penalty-area. Should the referee

a. award a penalty?
b. award a direct free-kick?
c. not stop play?

(Select the correct answer).

_____

If a match is extended to allow a penalty-kick to be taken, the extension will continue until:

1. the moment the ball passes wholly over the goal-line into goal, whether it goes directly into goal or rebounds from the goalpost into goal or is touched by the goal-keeper and goes into goal;
2. the moment the ball passes out of play outside the goalposts or over the crossbar;
3. the moment the ball is clearly saved by the goalkeeper or rebounds into play from the goalposts.

(Go straight on).

Which of the following statements is correct?

a. The upper edge of the crossbar has to be 8 feet from the ground.

b. The lower edge of the crossbar has to be 10 feet from the ground.

c. The lower edge of the crossbar has to be 8 feet from the ground.

Yes.

....

The linesman sees an offence by an attacker that takes place just before a goal was scored. The referee blows his whistle for a goal. The players kick-off. The linesman informs the referee of the offence. Should the referee

a. stop the game and cancel the goal?

b. allow play to continue?

(Select the correct answer).

No.

....

A player intentionally stops the ball with his arm but not his hand. Is this an offence?

———————————————————————

1. Re-take the kick.
2. Re-take the kick.

....

If necessary, the time of play shall be extended at half-time or full time to allow a penalty-kick to be taken.

The match will also be extended to allow the kick to be re-taken, if this is necessary because of an infringmeent by one of the players.

(Go straight on).

c. The lower edge of the crossbar has to be 8 feet from the ground.

....

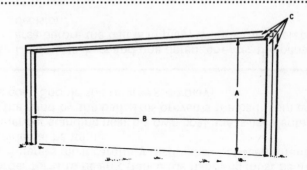

Give the distance marked A.
Give the distance marked B.
Give the maximum distance marked C.

---

b. allow play to continue as the game has re-started.

....

THE LINESMEN

Two linesmen are appointed for a match. The duties of linesmen are

1. to indicate when the ball is out of play;
2. if the ball is out of play, to indicate clearly which side is entitled to the throw-in, the corner-kick or the goal-kick;
3. to indicate a player is in an off-side position.

If the linesmen are neutral, they may draw the referee's attention to any breach of the laws of the game which they notice and which they believe the referee has not noticed. If the linesmen are club linesmen and not neutral, they will not normally have this power.

When a linesman draws an infringement to the attention of the referee, who decides what action is to be taken?

Penalty-kick.

....

It is an offence to handle the ball. Handling means carrying, striking or propelling the ball with any part of the hand or arm shaded in the diagram.

In order for it to be an offence the handling must be intentional. Referees must carefully distinguish between intentional and accidental handling.

A defender standing near his own goal-line is accidentally hit on the hand by the ball. This prevents the ball from entering the goal. Should the referee stop play?

---

1. If two attackers and one defender enter the penalty-area before the ball is in play, what is the referee's decision?

2. If an attacker enters the penalty-area before the ball is in play, and the ball is kicked into the goal, what is the referee's decision?

A = 8 feet; B = 8 yards; C = not more than 5 inches.

....

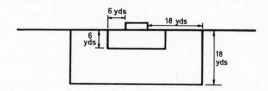

The goal-area lines are drawn 6 yards from the INSIDE of each goal-post and extend 6 yards into the field of play.

The penalty-area lines are drawn 18 yards from the INSIDE of each goal-post and extend 18 yards into the field of play.

In the goal-area the goalkeeper cannot be charged unless he is in possession of the ball.

In the penalty-area the goalkeeper is permitted to carry the ball, but if he holds the ball outside the penalty-area, he will be penalized for handling the ball.

(Go straight on).

The referee.

....

What are the three main functions of a linesman?

By a penalty-kick.

....

It is an offence to hold an opponent with one's arm or hand. This offence can happen if a player is held by any part of his body or clothes and when the arms of players are interlocked.

It is an offence to push a player with hand or arm. This offence includes cases where the goalkeeper pushes an opponent with the ball or throws the ball violently at an opponent.

A goalkeeper, in his own penalty-area, throws the ball violently into the face of an opponent. What is the referee's decision?

──

1. Caution the offender and award an indirect free-kick.
2. Goal-kick.

....

If a player or players from *both* sides enter the penalty-area before the ball is in play, the penalty-kick must be re-taken.

(Go straight on).

1. Will the goalkeeper be penalized for handling the ball in the goal-area?

2. If he runs into the penalty-area, can he be penalized for handling the ball?

3. If he runs beyond the penalty-area, can he be penalized for handling the ball?

---

1. To indicate when the ball is out of play.
2. To indicate which side is entitled to the throw-in, the corner, or the goal-kick.
3. To indicate that a player is in an off-side position.

....

If a linesman interferes unduly in the conduct of the game or if he gives insufficient assistance to the referee, the referee can send him off and arrange for a substitute. The referee will then report the linesman to the appropriate Affiliated Association.

(Go straight on).

It is an offence to strike or to attempt to strike an opponent.

The ball is in play near the centre of the field and the referee sees a defender in his own penalty-area strike an opponent. He considers this to be sufficiently violent conduct to send the player off. How would he re-start the game?

No.

....

1. An attacker enters the penalty-area before the ball is in play. The goalkeeper saves and the ball rebounds into play. What is the referee's decision?

2. An attacker enters the penalty-area before the ball is in play. The ball misses the goal and goes over the goal-line. What is the referee's decision?

1. No.
2. No.
3. Yes.

....

1. If the goalkeeper is in possession of the ball in the goal-area and he is charged by an attacking forward, would the forward be penalized?

2. If the goalkeeper is in possession of the ball in the penalty-area and he is charged by an attacking forward, would the forward be penalized?

_____

Under what circumstances can a linesman be sent off and reported?

1.

2.

1. Kicking or trying to kick an opponent.
2. Tripping an opponent.
3. Jumping at an opponent.
4. Charging an opponent in a violent or dangerous manner.
5. Charging an opponent from behind unless he is obstructing.

....

We shall now explain the four offences committed with the hands for which a direct free-kick or a penalty shall be awarded.

(Go straight on).

If an attacker, other than the kicker, enters the penalty-area before the ball is in play, the referee will first await the result of the kick.

If the ball goes into goal, the goal is disallowed and the kick re-taken. If the ball crosses the goal-line outside the goal, a goal-kick is awarded. If the ball rebounds into play from the goalkeeper or the goal-posts, the referee shall caution the offending attacker and award an indirect free-kick to the defending side.

Can a goal be scored from a penalty if an attacker has entered the penalty-area before the ball is in play?

1. No.
2. No.

....

THE BALL

The ball shall be spherical and have an outer casing of leather or other material approved by the International Board. Balls may be valve type or laced.

No material can be used in the construction of the ball that could be dangerous to the players.

If lacing is loose, could this be dangerous to the players?

──

1. For interfering too much in the conduct of the game.
2. For giving insufficient assistance to the referee.

....

Both the referee and the linesman, if they enter the field of play, are regarded as 'part of the field of play'. This means that if the ball hits them, play continues as if the ball had not touched them. Therefore, if the ball is kicked by an attacker, hits the referee and goes into the goal, then a goal has been scored.

If the ball rebounds from the referee and goes into touch, would a throw-in be taken?

b. allow the play to continue as no offence has been committed.

....

The three offences committed with the feet for which a direct free-kick or a penalty is awarded are:

1.
2.
3.

The two offences committed with the body for which a direct free-kick or a penalty is awarded are:

4.
5.

_____

b. The ball does not enter the goal.

....

We have seen that if a penalty-kick is awarded and a goal is scored from it, the referee will ignore any infringement by the goalkeeper and by the defending team and allow the goal.

Now we will explain what happens if one of the attacking team, other than the kicker, commits an offence when a penalty-kick is taken.

(Go straight on).

Yes.

....

At the start of the game the ball must be from 14 to 16 ounces in weight. The ball shall be not more than 28 inches and not less than 27 inches in circumference.

From what material can the outside covering of the ball be made?

_____

Yes.
Now turn to page 118 (bottom) for Post-Test on Section 2.

....

Section 3   The Kick-off, a Goal, the Throw-in, Goal-Kick, and Corner-Kick

THE KICK-OFF

At the start of the game and at the start of extra-time, if it is to be played, the captain winning the toss will choose either to kick-off or will choose the end of the field that his team will defend. If he should choose to kick-off, the other captain has the choice of ends. The teams will change ends at half-time.

The kick-off (a place kick) will take place from the centre of the field of play

1. at the start of the game and at the start of extra time;
2. after half-time;
3. after a goal has been scored.

(Go straight on).

Award a direct free-kick.

. . . .

It is an offence to charge an opponent from behind unless the latter is obstructing.

Player A deliberately turns his back on Player B and then does not attempt to play the ball. Player B charges him from behind. Should the referee

   a. penalize Player B?
   b. allow play to continue?

(Select the correct answer).

_____

Yes.

. . . .

The signal to take the kick has been given. One of the defenders, then, enters the penalty-area. The kick is taken. The referee will order the kick to be re-taken if

   a. the ball enters the goal
   b. the ball does not enter the goal.

(Select the correct answer).

Leather or other approved material.

....

The weight of the ball would be satisfactory if at the start of the game it weighed

  a. 12 ounces.
  b. 14 ounces.
  c. 19 ounces.

(Select the correct answer).

At the kick-off

1. every player must be in his own half of the field;
2. every player of the team opposing the kicker must remain at least 10 yards from the ball until it is kicked;
3. the ball must be kicked into the opposing half of the field;
4. the ball is not in play until it has travelled the distance of its own circumference;

If any of these rules are broken, the kick must be re-taken.

5. Once the ball is in play, the kicker shall not kick the ball a second time until it has been touched by another player.

If this rule is broken, an indirect free-kick is awarded at the place where the offence occured.

(Go straight on).

1. Kicking or trying to kick an opponent.

2. Tripping an opponent.

3. Jumping at an opponent.

....

It is an offence to charge an opponent in a *violent and dangerous manner.* Players may charge if the ball is within playing distance, if the charge is made fairly. The referee must judge whether a charge is made fairly or whether it is violent or dangerous. A fair charge is one where the player shoulders his opponent firmly but not violently.

Player A charges Player B by pushing with his elbow. The incident takes place near the left touchline. What action should the referee take?

1. Allow the goal.

2. The kick must be re-taken.

3. The kick must be re-taken.

....

If, after the signal to take the kick has been given, one of the defending side enters the penalty-area before the kick is taken, should the referee await the result of the kick?

b. 14 ounces.

....

The circumference of the ball must be

    a. 27 to 28 inches.
    b. 25 to 27 inches.
    c. 27 to 29 inches.

    (Select the correct answer).

    If the kicker plays the ball a second time, after it has travelled the distance of its circumfeernce, before it has been touched by another player, the referee shall

    a. award a direct free-kick;
    b. award an indirect free-kick;
    c. order the kick to be re-taken.

    (Select the correct answer).

No, the offence is jumping at an opponent, not at the ball.

....

We have explained the three offences committed with the feet for which a direct free-kick or a penalty is awarded. They are:

1.

2.

3.

---

b. Await the result of the kick.

....

The goalkeeper has moved and the referee has awaited the result of the kick.

1. If the kick is then taken and the ball enters the goal, what is the referee's decision?

2. If the kick is taken and the goalkeeper saves it, what is the referee's decision?

3. If the kick is taken and the ball goes over the goal-line but outside the goal, what is the referee's decision?

a. 27 to 28 inches.

....

1. What should the weight of the ball be at the start of the game?

2. What is the circumference of the ball?

---

b. an indirect free-kick.

....

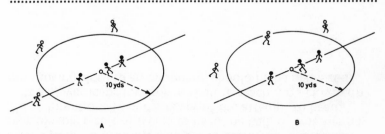

A   B

What infringements of the law are taking place in these diagrams of the kick-off and what action should be taken by the referee?

               Infringement   Action

A =

B =

It is an offence to jump at an opponent. Note that the offence is jumping at an opponent not at the ball. Again the referee must distinguish between an accidental and an intentional act.

Although it is impossible to jump at an opponent accidentally, it is not impossible to jump at the ball in order to head it and to crash into an opponent while doing so. The referee must judge whether a player, who crashes into an opponent after a jump to head the ball, did so accidentally and as an unavoidable result of trying to head the ball, or whether he did so intentionally under cover of the attempt to head.

If a player leaps towards the ball to reach it quickly without moving close to an opponent, should he be penalized?

Indirect free-kick as the kicker played the ball again before another player touched it.

....

If the goalkeeper or any of the defenders commits an offence when a penalty-kick is taken, the referee shall await the result of the kick. If the ball enters the goal, the referee shall allow the goal. If the ball does not enter the goal, the kick shall be re-taken.

If the goalkeeper moves his feet after the whistle for the kick but before the kick is taken, should the referee

   a. stop the game at once as the goalkeeper has moved his feet?
   b. await the result of the kick?

(Select the correct answer).

1. 14 to 16 ounces.
2. 27 to 28 inches.

....

It is possible that the ball may burst or become deflated during the match. If this should happen during the course of play, the referee must stop the game at once and re-start it by dropping the new ball at the place where the first ball burst.

If it should happen during a stoppage in the game, for example when the ball is in touch or over the goal line, the game is re-started with the new ball.

The ball bursts when a player kicks the ball towards the goal and the burst ball goes into the goal. Should the referee

a. allow the goal?
b. disallow the goal and re-start the game by dropping the new ball where the first ball burst?

(Select the correct answer).

A = Player not in own half.   Re-take kick.
B = Opposing player within 10 yards of ball.   Re-take kick.

....

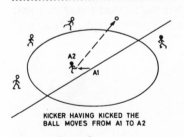

KICKER HAVING KICKED THE
BALL MOVES FROM A1 TO A2

C

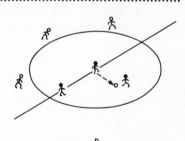

D

What infringements of the law are taking place in these diagrams of the kick-off and what action should be taken by the referee?

Infringement   Action

C =

D =

intentional.

....

The referee must also be careful to distinguish between a real trip and a pretended trip. A player may fall over, pretending that he has been tripped, in order to win a direct free-kick.

(Go straight on).

Goal—as the ball was kicked forward.

....

The kicker takes the penalty-kick and the ball hits a goalpost and rebounds to the kicker who kicks the ball into the goal. What is the referee's decision?

b. disallow the goal and re-start the game by dropping the new ball.

....

The ball goes over the touchline, hits the fence, and bursts. Should the referee

a. allow the throw-in with a new ball?
b. drop a new ball on the touchline?

(Select the correct answer).

─────────────────────────────────

C = Kicker kicks ball twice.   Indirect free-kick.
D = Kicking into own half of the field.   Re-take kick.

....

Therefore, for infringements at the kick-off the referee will order the kick to be re-taken except when the kicker kicks the ball a second time. If the kicker kicks the ball a second time, after it has travelled its own circumference, the referee shall award

a. a direct free-kick.
b. an indirect free-kick.

(Select the correct answer).

A direct free-kick as the kick was by an attacker in the penalty-area.

....

It is an offence to trip an opponent intentionally. The referee must be careful to distinguish between an intentional trip and an accidental trip resulting from normal play. For example if player A tackles player B and reaches the ball, player B might fall over player A's outstretched leg. This should not be penalized as player B tripped over in the normal and unavoidable course of play. The trip was not

_____.

The kick shall be re-taken.

....

The kicker takes the kick and rolls the ball gently forward. Another attacker runs forward after the ball is in play and shoots the ball into goal.
What is the referee's decision?

a. allow the throw-in with a new ball.

....

THE PLAYERS AND THEIR EQUIPMENT

The game is played by two teams, each with a maximum of 11 players one of whom must be a goalkeeper. The referee should notice which players are the goalkeepers but the positions played in by the other players are not the concern of the referee.

One of the other players can change places with the goalkeeper during the course of the match provided the referee is informed prior to the change. If the referee is not told, he will award a penalty-kick as soon as the player who has replaced the goalkeeper handles the ball in the penalty-area.

If the team captain wishes his right-back to change places with the goalkeeper, what should he do?

---

b. an indirect free-kick.

....

There are occasions when the play is re-started not by a kick-off but by the referee dropping the ball. This will happen after an injury or other temporary suspension when the game has been stopped while the ball is *still in play.*

The referee drops the ball and the ball is in play again when it has touched the ground. If a player commits an offence before the ball touches the ground, the player must be cautioned or sent off according the to seriousness of the offence. The referee shall drop the ball to re-start play.

Can the play be re-started by dropping the ball if the game was suspended while the ball was out of play?

a. a direct free-kick should be awarded.

....

It is an offence to kick intentionally or try to kick an opponent.

If an *attacking player* kicks a defender in the penalty-area, the referee must first decide if the kick was accidental or intentional. If he decides that it was intentional, what should he award?

When the ball has been kicked.

....

The kicker must not play the ball a second time until it has been touched by another player.

The kicker must kick the ball forward when taking a penalty-kick.

The player, taking the penalty-kick, kicked the ball back to one of his own team. What is the referee's decision?

Inform the referee.

....

During the course of a match substitutes are only allowed
in accordance with the Rules of the Competition.
Will a substitute be allowed to replace a player who is sent
off for violent conduct during the match?

No.

....

If play is re-started by the referee dropping the ball, when
is the ball in play?

1. intentionally.

2. by a defender.

3. in the penalty-area.

4. when the ball is in play.

....

We shall now examine the nine offences more closely. They can, however, only be fully understood if they are seen in practice. Remember that if one of them is committed outside the penalty-area, or inside the penalty-area by an attacker,

a. a direct free-kick should be awarded.
b. an indirect free-kick should be awarded.

(Select the correct answer).

1. On his own goal-line between the goal posts.

2. In the field of play outside the penalty-area and at least 10 yards from the ball.

....

When the penalty-kick is taken, the ball is in play directly it has been kicked forward and has travelled the distance of its own circumference.

When may the goalkeeper move his feet?

No.

....

Although during the course of the match substitutes are only allowed subject to the Rules of the competition, in all matches, a player who is sent off for violent conduct before the kick-off, can be replaced.

Which of these players could be replaced by a substitute?

a. A player who violently insults the referee before the start of the match and is sent off.

b. A player who is sent off shortly after half-time.

_____

When it has touched the ground.

....

If, when the referee drops the ball, a player commits an offence before the ball touches the ground,

1. what action should be taken against the offender by the referee?

2. how should the game be re-started?

b. a defender.
a. the ball is in play.

....

For a penalty-kick to be awarded all the following conditions must be fulfilled. One of the nine offences must have been committed

   1. intentionally

   2. by a_____

   3. in the_____

   4. when the ball is _____

---

  1. Where must the goalkeeper stand for the taking of a penalty-kick?

  2. Where must the other players stand for the taking of a penalty-kick?

a (when the Rules of the Competition permit).

....

The National or International Association must approve the rules concerning substitutes for players in competitive matches. In other matches agreement will be reached between the teams and the referee before the match subject to a maximum of two substitutes.

The Football Association rule is that before the start of a match a team can nominate *one* man who can be used as a substitute and the referee notified. The substitute can be used at any time in the match.

If the rules of the competition allow substitutes, is it normal in England

   a. for any number of permissible players to be replaced by substitutes?
   b. for one player to be replaced by a substitute?

(Select the correct answer).

_____

1. The player shall be cautioned or sent off.
2. The ball shall be dropped again.

....

   1. At the kick-off the kicker passes the ball backwards. What action is taken?

   2. At the kick-off the kicker kicks the ball a second time after it has travelled its own circumference. What is the penalty?

   3. At the kick-off an opposing player advanced within 10 yards of the ball before it was kicked. What action is taken?

   4. A player is seriously injured and the referee stops play when the ball is still in play. How is the game re-started?

   5. If extra-time is played, which side kicks off in extra-time?

A penalty, as the act took place in the penalty-area.

....

For a penalty-kick to be awarded, one of the nine offences must have been committed intentionally in the penalty-area by

a. an attacker.
b. a defender.

while

a. the ball is in play.
b. the ball is in or out of play.

(Select the correct answers).

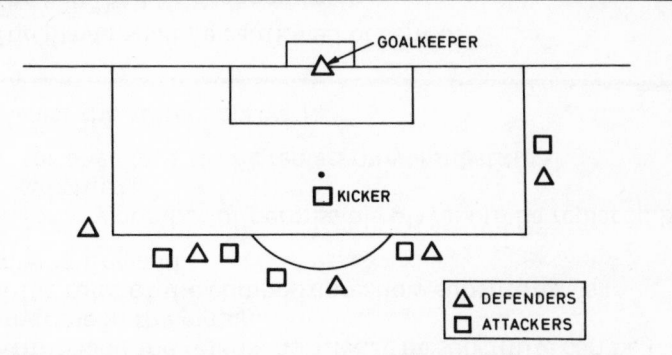

Apart from the player taking the kick and the opposing goalkeeper, all players must be in the field of play, outside the penalty-area and at least 10 yards from the ball i.e. beyond the restraining arc. They need not, however, be behind the ball.

The goalkeeper must stand on his own goal-line without moving his feet until the ball is kicked.

It is necessary that all players are correctly positioned before the kick is taken and the referee should not give the signal for the kick until the players are in position.

(Go straight on).

b. for one player to be replaced by a substitute.

....,...............

In competitive matches

a. substitutes will always be allowed
b. substitutes will only be allowed if the rules of the competition approved by the National or International Association permit.

(Select the correct answer).

---

1. Re-take the kick.

2. Indirect free-kick.

3. Re-take the kick.

4. By dropping the ball.

5. As decided by the captain winning the toss.

(Go straight on).

b. award a penalty.

....

A defender, not the goalkeeper, standing outside the penalty-area, stretches and intentionally handles the ball inside the penalty-area. What should the referee award?

___

1. Caution the players.

2. Caution the players for ungentlemanly conduct.

3. Indirect free-kick for opposing side.

4. Re-take the kick.

....

PENALTY-KICKS

When a penalty has been awarded for one of the nine offences that are punished by a penalty, the penalty-kick is taken from the penalty-mark.

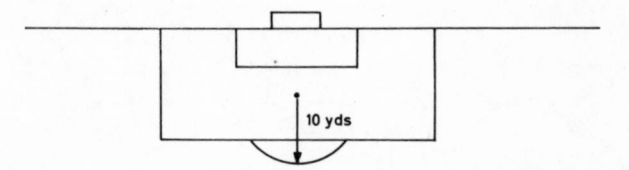

Note the restraining arc drawn 10 yards from the penalty-mark.

(Go straight on).

b. Substitutes will only be allowed if the Rules of the National or International Association and Competitions permit.

....

Players normally wear shirts or jerseys, shorts, stockings, and boots. The goalkeepers' jerseys should be of colours which clearly distinguish them from other players.

Players must not wear anything that could cause injury to other players. Because of this there are clear regulations concerning the boots that can be worn.

Studs must be made of leather, rubber, aluminium, plastic, or other similar material and they must be solid. No metal plates can be worn even if they are covered with leather or rubber. If the stud is of the screw type and needs metal seating, the metal seating must be embedded in the sole of the boot. If the stud is of the screw type, the screw must be part of the stud and be screwed into the boot and not part of the boot and screwed into the stud. Studs should not have any protruding rims or edges.

All these rules are to prevent_____to other players.

A GOAL—OR IS IT?

In order for a goal to be scored, the WHOLE of the ball must pass over the goal-line under the crossbar and between the posts.

Which of the balls in the diagram show that a goal has been scored?

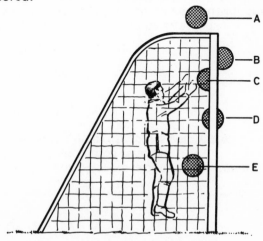

intentional.

....

   If any of the nine offences is committed intentionally, then a direct free-kick should be awarded.
   But if any of the nine offences is committed

   1. intentionally;

   2. in the penalty-area;

   3. by a defender;

   4. while the ball is in play;

then a PENALTY-KICK should be awarded.
   This is so even though the ball may be outside the penalty-area when the offence is committed.
   If a defender strikes an opponent in the penalty-area when the ball is near the halfway line, should the referee

   a. award a direct free-kick where the ball is?
   b. award a penalty?

   (Select the correct answer).

_____

What decisions should the referee take if

   1. an opponent does not retire ten yards from the ball when a free-kick is being taken?

   2. opponents jump about in front of the kicker to distract him?

   3. the kicker plays the ball a second time before it has been touched by another player?

   4. the ball does not travel the length of its circumference after the kick?

injury.

....

Which of the following studs would be passed as satisfactory?

a. Leather studs with metal plates covered by leather.
b. Leather, screw type studs with the screw as part of the boot screwed into the stud.
c. Aluminium, screw type studs with the screw as part of the stud and screwed into the boot.

E only.

....

Have goals been scored in the situations shown in the diagrams?

In diagram A the ball hits the underside of the crossbar and bounces out.

In diagram B the goalkeeper catches the ball and kicks it up the field.

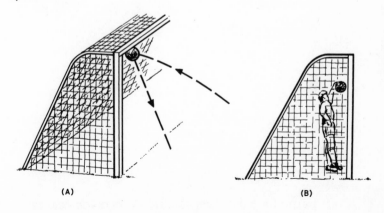

(A)   (B)

b. let play go on as no offence has been committed.

....

So when a player does an act which could be one of the nine offences for which a direct free-kick is awarded, the first thing the referee must do is to decide whether the act was

_____.

━━

1. Re-take the kick.

2. Corner.

....

The ball must be stationary when a free-kick is taken, and the kicker must not play the ball a second time until it has been touched by another player. If the player plays the ball again before it has been touched by another player, the referee shall award an indirect free-kick to the opposing side.

If, when a free-kick is being taken, any of the players gesticulate or try to distract their opponents, the referee shall caution the offending players for ungentlemanly conduct.

c. Aluminium, screw type studs . . . etc.
....

Look at the diagram of studs. Note that

1. studs must be round in plan;

2. the diameter must not be less than ½ inch even when the stud is tapered;

3. if there is a base, the base must not protrude more than ¼ inch.

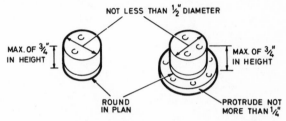

NOT LESS THAN ½" DIAMETER

MAX. OF ¾" IN HEIGHT

MAX. OF ¾" IN HEIGHT

ROUND IN PLAN

PROTRUDE NOT MORE THAN ¼"

What is the maximum distance that a stud or a stud and base can protrude from the sole or heel of a boot?

A = No.
B = Yes.

....

A goal cannot be scored direct from a throw-in, from the kick-off, from a goal-kick, or from an indirect free-kick.

A goal cannot be scored if the ball is thrown, carried or pushed into the goal by an attacker using his arm or hand unless the attacker is the opposing goalkeeper throwing from his own penalty-area.

If the goalkeeper clears the ball by throwing it from his own penalty-area and the ball goes the length of the field into the opponents' goal, would a goal be awarded?

Yes.

....

For any of the *nine* offences to be penalized, it must have been committed *intentionally*.

If a player accidently touches the ball with his hand, should the referee

a. award a direct free-kick?

b. let play go on as no offence has been committed?

(Select the correct answer).

────────────────────────────

1. A player takes an indirect free-kick inside his own penalty-area and kicks the ball back to his goalkeeper. The goalkeeper misses it and the ball goes into the goal. What is the referee's decision?

2. A player, taking a free-kick outside his penalty-area, kicks the ball back to his goalkeeper. The goalkeeper misses it and the ball goes into the goal. What is the referee's decision?

¾ inch.

....

1. What must be the shape of studs in plan?

2. What is the minimum diameter of a stud that is permitted?

3. If there is a base to the stud, how far may the base protrude?

Yes.

....

Can a goal be scored direct from

1. the kick-off?

2. a corner?

3. a goal-kick?

4. a throw-in?

5. an indirect free-kick?

OFFENCES FOR WHICH A DIRECT FREE-KICK OR A PENALTY IS AWARDED.

A direct free-kick is awarded against a player who intentionally commits any of the following *nine* offences:

1. Kicking or attempting to kick an opponent. ⎫
2. Tripping an opponent.   ⎬ 3 with the feet
3. Jumping at an opponent.   ⎭
4. Charging an opponent in a violent or a dangerous manner. ⎫
5. Charging an opponent from behind unless he is obstructing. ⎬ 2 with the body ⎭
6. Striking or attempting to strike an opponent. ⎫
7. Holding an opponent.   ⎬ 4 with the hands
8. Pushing an opponent.   ⎪
9. Handling the ball.   ⎭

Before stopping play for any of these offences, can the referee consider playing the advantage clause?

Outside the penalty-area and at least 10 yards from the ball.

....

If a player takes a free-kick from inside his own penalty-area, the goalkeeper shall not receive the ball into his hands in order to clear the ball up the field.

If the player taking the kick from inside his own penalty-area, kicks the ball into his own goal or over the goal-line without the ball leaving the penalty-area, the kick is re-taken.

If a player takes a free-kick from outside his penalty-area and the ball goes into his own goal, the referee shall award a corner.

(Go straight on).

1. Round.
2. ½ inch.
3. ¼ inch.

....

If bars are used under the boot, the bars must be made of leather or rubber, they must be flat and set across the width of the boot. The bars must be not less than ½ inch in width, have rounded corners and extend right across the width of the boot.

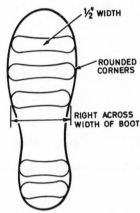

Bars, like studs, must not protrude more than_____ from the sole or heel of the boot.

1. No.   4. No.
2. Yes.   5. No.
3. No.

....

If a defending player, other than the goalkeeper intentionally handles the ball and prevents it entering the goal, the referee must award a penalty if the handling takes place in the penalty-area.

However, if the defending player handles the ball but fails to stop it and the ball enters the goal, the goal is allowed.

(Go straight on).

We shall deal with the laws concerning fouls and misconduct in four sections according to the punishment that the referee awards.

1. Offences for which a direct free-kick or a penalty is awarded.

2. Offences for which an indirect free-kick is awarded.

3. Offences for which a player should be cautioned.

4. Offences for which a player should be sent off.

(Go straight on).

---

b. the ball has not passed beyond the penalty-area.

....

Where must opposing players stand if a free-kick is being taken by a player inside his own penalty-area?

¾ inch.

....

1. May bars extend beyond the width of the boots?
2. May bars have squared edges?

1. The defending right-back touches the ball with his hand in a desperate attempt to stop a goal. The ball goes on into the goal. What is the referee's decision?
2. The defending right-back succeeds in stopping the ball with his hand in the penalty-area. The ball would have gone into the goal. What is the referee's decision?

An indirect free-kick.

Now turn to page 177 (top) for Post-Test on Section 4.

....

Section 5   Fouls and Misconduct

It is of great importance that both players and referee should learn and fully understand the laws concerning fouls and misconduct. The spirit in which these laws are taken is vital to the success of the match.

Players should remember:

1. To accept the referee's decision without question.

2. Not to retaliate when fouled.

3. To keep their temper.

4. To refrain from claiming for 'hands' or any other infringement.

Referees should remember:

1. To use their powers firmly and impartially.

2. To reach their decision quickly.

3. That they should play the advantage clause, but that to keep control is essential.

(Go straight on).

_____

Caution the two players.

....

When a player is taking an indirect or a direct free-kick from *inside* his own penalty-area, the opposing players must stand at least 10 yards from the ball and outside the penalty-area until the ball is in play. The ball is in play when it has travelled the length of its circumference. If the ball is not kicked direct into play, the kick must be re-taken.

When a player takes the kick from inside his penalty-area, the kick will be re-taken if

a. the ball has not travelled the distance of its own circumference

b. the ball _____
(Complete the sentence)

1. No.

2. No.

....

Combined bars and studs may be worn. Look at the diagram and note that

1. the minimum width of the bar is ½ inch;

2. the bar and studs together must not protrude more than ¾ inch from the sole or heel of the boot;

3. the studs must be round in plan and have a minimum diameter of ½ inch.

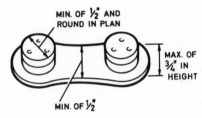

The bars must run

a. along the length of the boot
b. across the width of the boot.

(Select the correct answer).

━━━━━━━━━━━━━━━━━━━━━━━━━━━━━━━━━

1. Goal.

2. Penalty.

....

The referee, as you know, is regarded as part of the field of play. If the outside-right centres the ball and it hits the referee and rebounds into the goal, what is the referee's decision?

1. He must not interfere with play in any way.
2. No, he is not influencing the play.

....

What is the penalty for being off-side?

―――――――――――――――――――――――――――

1. At least 10 yards from the ball or on their own goal-line between the goalposts.
2. When it has travelled the distance of its own circumference.

....

A free-kick has been awarded and two of the opposing players are standing about 5 yards from the ball hoping to delay the kick until their colleagues are in position. What is the referee's decision?

b. across the width of the boot.

....

It is the duty of the referee to see that the boots and other equipment of the players conform to the laws. Before International Matches and International Competitions, and before League and Competition Matches, if their rules require it, the referee inspects the boots and equipment before the match or at half-time. If at any time during the match the referee believes that boots may be at fault, he may look at the player's boots at once.

If the referee notices that a player has scratches on his legs which could have been caused by boot-nails, what should he do?

A goal.

....

A goal is not allowed if the ball was prevented from crossing the line by a spectator or other 'outside agency'. If this happens, the game must be stopped and restarted by the referee dropping the ball at the place where the interference took place. However, if a spectator tried but failed to stop the ball crossing the line, the goal would be allowed.

(Go straight on).

Yes, as the defender is distracted by $\boxed{C}$ and is being prevented from covering $\boxed{B}$.

....

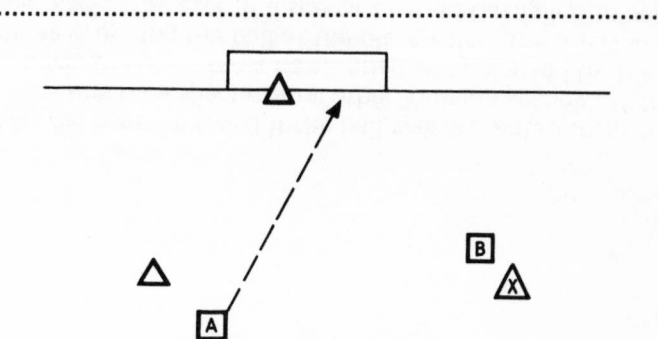

1. $\boxed{A}$ shoots at goal and $\boxed{B}$, who is off-side, prevents defender $\triangle\!\!\!\!_{X}$ from running to intercept the ball. $\boxed{B}$ should be penalized for off-side. Why?

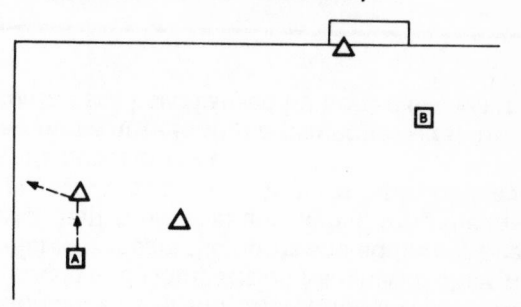

2. $\boxed{B}$ is off-side. $\boxed{A}$ kicks the ball which hits a defender and is deflected towards touch. Should $\boxed{B}$ be penalized?

---

1. Where should opposing players stand when a free-kick is being taken?

2. When is the ball in play after a player has taken a free-kick from a spot outside his own penalty-area?

Inspect the boots of the players.

....

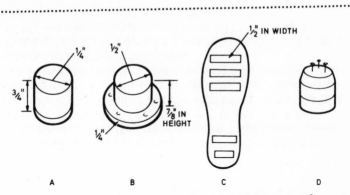

A   B   C   D

The diagrams show studs or bars which do not conform to the laws.

Write down the fault in each diagram.

Fault

A. =

B. =

C. =

D. =

---

1. For a goal to be scored the_____ball must cross the line between the post and under the crossbar.
2. A goalkeeper catches the ball in front of the line but falls over backwards carrying the ball behing the line. Is it a goal?
3. Taking a throw-in, a player throws the ball direct into his opponent's goal. What is the referee's decision?
4. The ball is rolling slowly towards the goal-line when it is stopped by the goalkeeper's cap which has fallen off. What is the referee's decision?
5. The ball is travelling towards the goal. An angry but drunk spectator rushes on to the field, tries to stop it but misses and the ball goes into the net. What is the referee's decision?

Yes.

....

A passes to B who is unmarked. C is clearly off-side. Note the position of the defender next to C and state whether you think C should be penalized for influencing the play.

By raising one arm above his head.

....

When a player is taking a direct or an indirect free-kick outside his own penalty-area, opposing players must stand at least ten yards from the ball until it is in play. The ball is in play when it has travelled the distance of its own circumference. If the free-kick is being taken from a spot less than ten yards from their goal-line, the opposing players may stand on their goal-line between the posts.

Players who do not retire ten yards from the spot where the kick is taken, should be cautioned. If they repeat the offence, they should be sent off.

(Go straight on).

A = Diameter only ¼ inch.

B = Height is ⅞ inch which is too high.

C = Bars have square edges and do not extend across the width of the boot.

D = Nails sticking out.

....

If a player's boot or equipment are at fault, the referee must send him off the field at once to adjust his boots or equipment. When the player has corrected the fault, he can only re-enter the field of play

    1. during a stoppage, and

    2. after he has reported to the referee who will see that the boots or equipment are now in order.

Can a player re-enter the field and report to the referee when the ball is in touch?

---

1. Whole.

2. Yes.

3. No goal—goal-kick.

4. Stop the game and re-start by dropping the ball.

5. Goal.

....

BALL OUT OF PLAY—THE THROW-IN, THE GOAL-KICK, AND THE CORNER-KICK

Remember that the lines belong to the areas of which they are the boundaries. Therefore the goal-line itself and the touchline itself (are/are not) part of the field of play.

No.

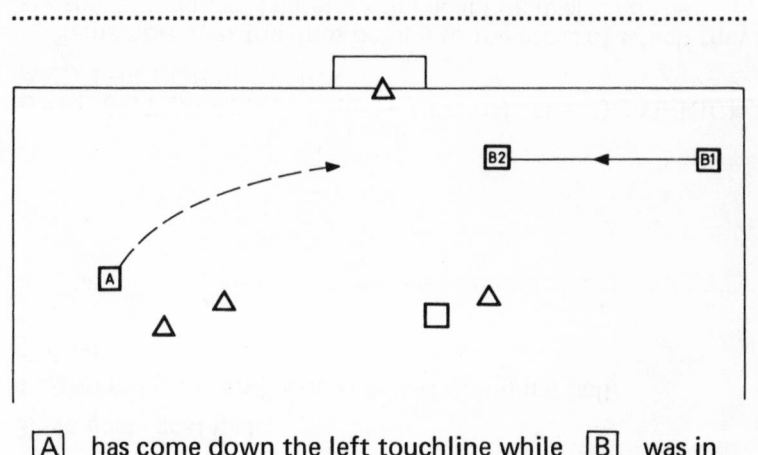

A has come down the left touchline while B was in position B1. Although B was off-side here he was too far away from play to be influencing it. B then runs in to position B2 as A centres the ball. Now B has become a factor in the game and is influencing it. Should he be penalized?

b. a goal-kick.

The referee should ensure that a free-kick is taken as quickly as possible so that the game is not slowed down, and so as to prevent the offending side from gaining the benefit of being able to rearrange its defence.

As you have learned, when awarding a direct free-kick the referee blows his whistle but when awarding an indirect free-kick he blows his whistle and signals. How does he signal?

Yes.

....

If a player re-enters the field while play is in progress, the referee shall stop the game, unless by doing so the offending player gains an advantage. He should then caution the player and restart the game by dropping the ball.

When and how may a player return to the field?

_____

are.

....

The ball is out of play

1. when the WHOLE of the ball has crossed the WHOLE of the touchline or the WHOLE of the goal-line,

2. when the game has been stopped by the referee.

Therefore

1. if the ball rolls along the goal-line or touchline without wholly crossing it, the ball is (in play/out of play);

2. if the ball hits the goalpost or the corner flag and rebounds into the field of play, the ball is (in play/out of play);

3. if the players think that there has been an infringement but the referee does not blow his whistle, the ball is (in play/out of play);

4. if the ball strikes the flagpost at the halfway line, the ball is (in play/out of play).

(Select the correct answers).

Yes.

....

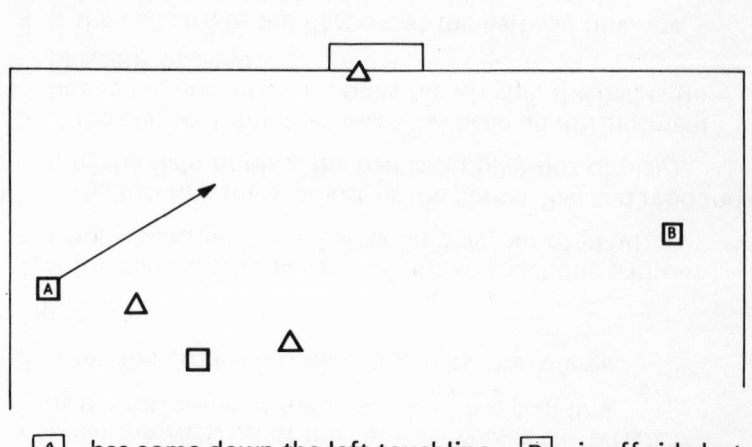

A has come down the left touchline. B is off-side but he is too far away from the play to be influencing it. Should B be penalized?

A player takes an indirect free-kick and the ball goes directly into the opponents' goal. Should the referee award

a. a goal?
b. a goal-kick?

(Select the correct answer).

During a stoppage after he has reported to the referee.

....

If a player returns during play, the referee should stop the game and

a. award an indirect free-kick,
b. caution the player.

(Select the correct answer).

_____

1. in play.

2. in play.

3. in play.

4. out of play.

....

Which of the balls A, B, and C is out of play?

FIELD OF PLAY

TOUCH LINE

A   B   C

It is clear that he will be interfering with play if he plays the ball. We shall illustrate the other ways in which he can influence play.

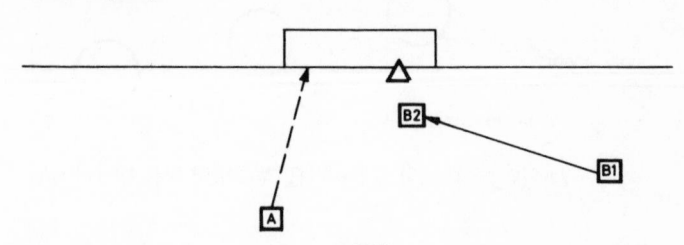

B is off-side in position B1. He runs in towards position B2 as A shoots at goal. He distracts the goal-keeper by running and prevents him playing the ball properly Should he be penalized?

Section 6 Free-Kicks and Penalties

FREE-KICKS

There are two types of free-kick:

1. DIRECT free-kick, from which a goal can be scored direct against the offending team.
2. INDIRECT free-kick, from which a goal cannot be scored directly against the offending team. The ball must be touched by another player, other than the kicker, before going into the goal in order for a goal to be scored. If the ball goes directly into the opponents' goal from an indirect free-kick, the referee shall award a goal-kick.

(Go straight on).

b. caution the player.

....

If the game has been stopped because a player has returned to the field while play is in progress, how should the referee re-start play?

C.
....

If a ball goes wholly out of play while in the air but then swerves back to bounce in the field of play, the ball is (in play/ out of play)?

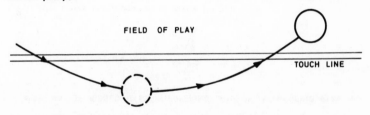

INTERFERING WITH OR INFLUENCING PLAY

A PLAYER MAY BE JUDGED TO BE INTERFERING WITH OR INFLUENCING PLAY IF —

– He plays the ball

–He moves into a position to receive the ball

–He is distracting a defender because
his position is potentially threatening

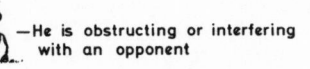

–He is obstructing or interfering
with an opponent

(Go straight on).

1. Playing in a manner the referee considers to be dangerous.

2. Charging an opponent fairly when the opponent is not within playing distance of the ball.

3. Intentionally obstructing an opponent.

4. Charging the goalkeeper when he is inside his goal-area provided that he is not holding the ball and he is not obstructing.

5. When the goalkeeper is 'carrying' the ball.

Now turn to Post-Test on Section 5, page 238.

By dropping the ball.
Now turn to page 61 (top) for Post-Test on Section 1

....

Section 2 The Referee and the Linesmen

A Referee shall be appointed for each game. When on the field of play it is advisable that the referee should have two whistles, two watches, a coin, pencil, and paper. The ball must be approved by the referee before the game commences.

Do you think that a referee should wear clothes that distinguish him from other players?

Out of play.

....

If the ball hits the referee and remains in the field of play, the ball is still in play and the game goes on.

If the ball goes over the line it is for the referee to signal that the ball is out of play. If the referee is uncertain he can consult the linesman.

If the linesman signals that the ball has gone out of play but the referee does not whistle, the players should

a. play on,
b. stop.

(Select the correct answer).

1. he is in his own half of the field.

2. there are two opponents nearer to the goal-line than he is.

3. the ball was last touched by an opponent.

4. he received the ball direct from a goal-kick, a corner-kick, a throw-in, or when it was dropped by the referee.

....

You now know when a player is off-side. The punishment for being off-side is an indirect free-kick taken from the place where the player was off-side. However, a player who is in an off-side position should NOT ALWAYS BE PENALIZED.

A player who is in an off-side position should only be penalized if he is interfering with or influencing the game.

The referee then has these stages to his decision.

IS THE PLAYER IN AN OFF-SIDE POSITION? Yes.
IS HE INTERFERING WITH OR
INFLUENCING PLAY?
    Yes—PENALIZE
    No—DO NOT PENALIZE.   (Go straight on)

_____

Yes.

....

List five offences for which an indirect free-kick should be awarded.

Yes, this is important as regards his jacket and stockings.

....

What things, necessary for carrying out his duties, should the referee have with him on the field of play?

_____

a. play on, as only the referee can give the decision.

....

1. The ball is out of play when

    a. the_____of the line has been crossed by the _____of the ball.
    b. when the game has been_____by the referee.

2. If the ball rebounds into the field of play after hitting the referee or the corner flag or the goalposts, the ball is (in play/out of play).

1. No, he has received the ball direct from a throw-in.
2. No, the ball was last touched by an opponent.

....

You have learned that a player is off-side if he is nearer his opponent's goal-line than the ball at the moment the ball is played, unless

1._____

2._____

3._____

4. the ball was received direct from _____

An indirect free-kick.

....

The two offences involving the goalkeeper for which an indirect free-kick is awarded are

1. Charging the goalkeeper when he is inside his own goal-area provided that he is not holding the ball and he is not obstructing.

2. When the goalkeeper 'carries the ball' more than four steps.

If a goalkeeper takes three steps with the ball, touches the ground with the ball and takes another three steps with it, should the referee penalize him?

A whistle, a watch, a coin, pencil, and paper.

....

THE AUTHORITY OF THE REFEREE

The duties and powers of a referee under the Laws of the Game are as follows:

1. To keep a record of the game and to act as timekeeper.

2. To enforce the Laws and decide disputed points.

3. He has discretionary power to stop the game for any infringement of the Laws.

4. He has discretionary power to suspend the game.

5. He has discretionary power to caution a player for misconduct or ungentlemanly behaviour.

6. He has discretionary power to send a player off the field for the rest of the game.

7. To allow no-one except the players and linesmen on the field without his permission.

8. To stop the game for serious injury.

9. To signal for the game to restart after stoppages.

10. To approve the ball and the players' equipment.

We shall explain these duties and powers in more detail.

(Go straight on).

_____

1. *a.* whole .... whole.
   b. stopped.
2. in play.

....

THE THROW-IN

When the ball goes out of play over the touchline, it is thrown in from the place where it crossed the line by a player of the team opposing the player who put the ball out of play.

The linesman shows the place from which the throw is to be taken and signals the team that is to take the throw.

If players think that the linesman is giving the throw to the wrong team, should they complain to the referee?

129305.

1. a goal-kick.
2. a corner-kick.
3. a throw-in.

....

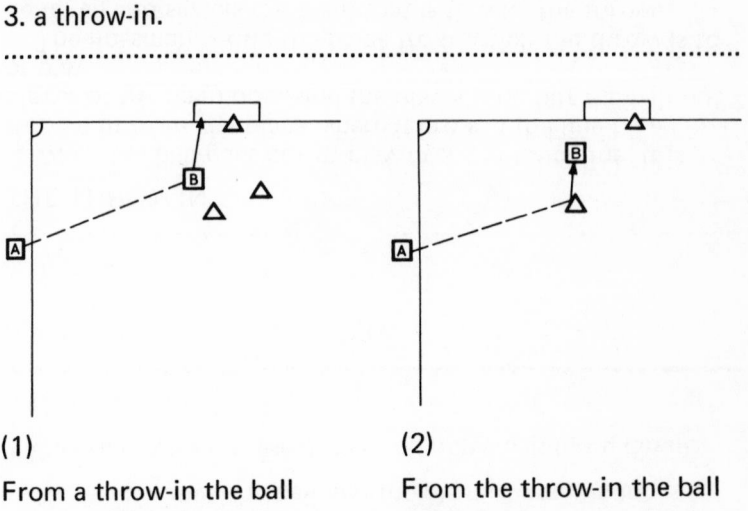

(1)

From a throw-in the ball goes to [B] who has only one opponent between him and the goal-line. Is [B] off-side? Give the reason for your answer.

(2)

From the throw-in the ball glances off an opponent and goes to [B] who scores. Is [B] off-side? Give the reason for your answer.

_____

1. When he is inside his own goal-area;
2. provided he is not holding the ball;
3. and provided that he is not obstructing.

....

The goalkeeper is allowed to carry the ball but he must not take more than four steps without releasing it so that it is played by another player. If a goalkeeper takes more than four steps without releasing the ball, he shall be penalized for 'carrying' and_____free-kick shall be awarded.

The referee's authority begins as soon as he enters the field of play and his powers to penalize extend to offences committed when the ball is out of play and when the play has been temporarily suspended (e.g. half-time).

Can the referee penalize for an offence committed:

1. During a stoppage for injury?—Yes/No

2. During the half-time?—Yes/No

3. While the ball is over the goal-line?—Yes/No

No, they should keep quiet and follow the linesman's decision.

....

When throwing in, the player must

1. face the field of play;

2. keep part of each foot in contact with the ground on or behind the touchline;

3. throw the ball from behind and over his head;

4. use both hands for the throw.

If there is an infringement of any of these rules, the throw must be re-taken by the opposing team.

If the thrower uses one hand for throwing and the other to guide the throw, would it be a foul throw?

1. No, because he received the ball direct from a corner.

2. Yes, because he did not receive the ball direct from a corner.

....

A player cannot be off-side if he receives the ball direct from

1._____

2._____

3._____

4. when it is dropped by the referee.

━━━━━━━━━━━━━━━━━━━━━━━━━━━━━━━━━━━━━

1. No, as the goalkeeper is holding the ball.

2. No, as the goalkeeper is obstructing.

....

It is an offence to charge the goalkeeper

1. When he is inside his own _____.

2. Provided he is not _____.

3. And provided he is not_____.

1. Yes.

2. Yes.

3. Yes.

....

The referee's authority and his use of discretionary powers begin as soon as he enters the field of play. Discretionary powers are powers that he can use on his own judgement, or at his own discretion.

The referee has come on to the field and is walking towards the centre circle. One of the players comes up to him and shouts violent abuse at him and accuses him of unfairness. Could the referee send the player off the field for the rest of the game?

Yes, both hands must be used for a throw.

....

In the diagrams below both feet are on the ground. In which diagrams would there be a foul throw because of the position of the feet?

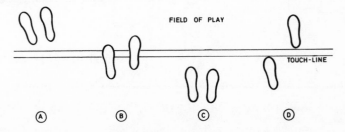

Yes.
No.

....

Look at the diagrams.

(1)   (2)

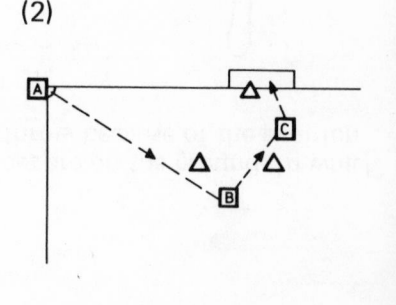

[A] takes the corner and   [A] takes the corner and
the ball goes to [B] who   the ball goes to [B] who
only has one opponent   passes to [C] who scores.
between him and the goal-   Is [C] off-side? Give the
line. Is [B] off-side? Give   reason for your answer.
the reason for your answer.

─────────────────────────────────────

No.

....

'1. The goalkeeper is holding the ball in his goal-area and
    an opposing forward charges him fairly. Is this an offence?

 2. The goalkeeper drops the ball and then stands between
    the forward and the ball in an attempt to stop the forward
    reaching the ball. Is it an offence for the forward to
    charge him now?

Yes.

....

As you learned when substitutes were explained, a player who is sent off before the start of the game (can be replaced/cannot be replaced) by another player.

(Select the correct answer).

_____

A and D.

....

1. Can the thrower throw the ball in underarm?

2. Can the thrower throw the ball in over his head with one hand?

3. What is the penalty for a foul throw?

No, because the ball was last played by a defender.

....

Exception 4. *A player cannot be off-side if he receives the ball* DIRECT *from a goal-kick, a corner-kick, a throw-in or when it is dropped by the referee.*

Note that he must receive the ball direct, and that the list does not include free-kicks and penalties.

1. A player receives the ball direct from a *free-kick* and is in front of the ball with no opponents between himself and the goal-line. Is he off-side?

2. If he had received the ball direct from a corner, would he have been off-side?

_____

1. Playing in a way that the referee considers to be dangerous.

2. Charging fairly when the opponent is not within playing distance of the ball.

3. Intentionally obstructing the opponent.

....

There are two other offences for which an indirect free-kick is awarded and involving the goalkeeper.

First, it is an offence to charge the goalkeeper when he is inside his goal-area, except when he is holding the ball or obstructing an opponent.

Is it an offence to charge the goalkeeper fairly when he has moved *outside* his goal-area?

Can be replaced.

....

THE DUTY OF THE REFEREE TO KEEP A RECORD OF THE GAME AND TO ACT AS TIMEKEEPER.

The referee should keep a record of the game and note the goals scored. He must also carefully time the two halves of the match and the half-time period. Matches *normally* have two equal periods of 45 minutes unless the rules of the competition state that play is for less time. The half-time period, to which the players have a RIGHT, shall not be longer than 5 minutes unless the referee allows.

If the captains agree to forego the half-time interval but one of the players insists on having the interval, what should the referee do?

━━━

1. No.

2. No.

3. The opposing team re-takes the throw.

....

The ball is in play as soon as it is thrown across the line into the field of play. However, the thrower cannot play the ball again until it has been touched by another player.

If the thrower plays the ball again before it is touched by another player, the referee shall award an *indirect* free-kick.

If the thrower HANDLES the ball again after it has returned to play, the referee shall award a *direct* free-kick.

(Go straight on).

Because it was last played by an opponent.

....

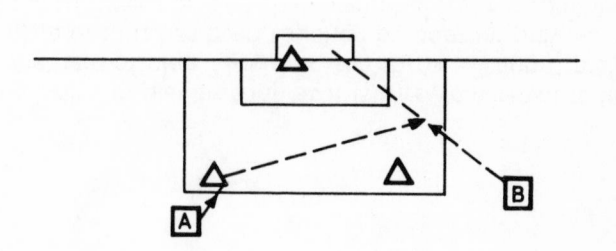

A shoots, the ball glances off a defender's foot and goes to B who scores.

Is B off-side?

Give the reason for your answer.

_____

Indirect free-kick for obstruction.

....

You have learnt of three offences for which an indirect free-kick should be awarded. What are they?

1.

2.

3.

He must allow the half-time interval as players have a right to it.

....

1. What is the normal duration of a match?

2. What is the normal time allowed at half-time?

3. Must the match be divided into two equal periods?

_____

What action should the referee take over the following infringements concerned with the throw-in?

1. The thrower plays the ball a second time before it is touched by another player.

2. The thrower is not facing the field of play.

3. The thrower has one foot over the line.

4. The thrower handles the ball after it has returned to the field of play.

5. The thrower throws the ball and the ball does not enter the field of play.

Exception 3. A player cannot be off-side if the ball was last *touched or played by an opponent.*

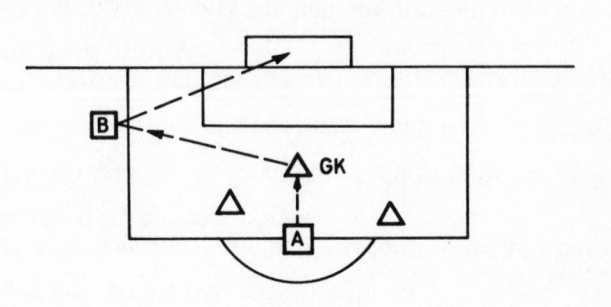

[A] shoots, the referee having decided that B is not inter-fering with the play; the ball is played out by the goalkeeper who has advanced but [B] gets possession and scores. Note that [B] was in front of the ball and did not have two opponents between him and the goal-line. However, he is not off-side? Why

___

No, because he is playing the ball.

....

A defender kicks the ball towards the goal-line. An attacker, hoping for a corner, moves between the defender and the ball without attempting to play the ball and prevents the defender from kicking the ball again. What should the referee's decision be?

1. Two equal periods of 45 minutes.

2. Five minutes.

3. Yes.

....

There are two occasions when the referee should add time
to the end of the first or second half.

1. If time has been lost through injury or other cause, the
   referee should add time to the end of the half. The
   amount added is the same as the amount lost.

2. If a penalty-kick is awarded just before the end of the
   half, time should be allowed to take the penalty-kick.

If two minutes are lost because a player has been injured
in the first half, should time be added at the end

a. of the first half?
b. of the match?

(Select the correct answer).

_____

1. Indirect free-kick.

2. Opposing team re-takes the throw.

3. Opposing team re-takes the throw.

4. Direct free-kick.

5. Re-take the throw.

....

A goal cannot be scored directly from a throw-in. Therefore,
if the thrower throws the ball directly into his opponents'
goal, the referee awards a goal-kick. If the thrower throws
the ball directly into his own goal, the referee awards a
corner.

(Go straight on).

1. Yes, he did not have two opponents between him and the goal-line when [A] centred.
2. Yes, there are not two opponents between him and the goal-line.

....

You have now learned that a player cannot be off-side when

1. he is in his own half;

2. there are two opponents nearer to their own goal-line than he is at the moment that the ball is played.

Look back at the diagrams on the last five pages and make certain that you understand the problems. Then go straight on.

―――――――――――――――――――――――――

Because Player B was not in playing distance of the ball.

....

When a player is not playing the ball it is an offence intentionally to obstruct an opponent. Obstruction would include:

—running between the opponent and the ball with the intention of preventing him reaching it.
—putting oneself in front of an opponent so as to shield a colleague or the ball without attempting to play the ball.

It is only an offence to obstruct when one is not playing the ball. If a player is dribbling the ball and is challenged by an opponent, would it be an offence if he turned his back on his opponent in order to shield the ball?

a. at the end of the first half.

....

If, 30 seconds from the end of full-time, a player commits an infringement for which a penalty-kick should be given, would the referee

    a. end the game at the end of the 30 seconds?
    b. allow the penalty-kick to be taken first?

(Select the correct answer).

_____

1. The thrower throws the ball in correctly and then runs forward and handles it. What is the referee's decision?

2. The ball is thrown directly into the opponents' goal. What is the referee's decision?

3. Give three examples of a foul throw.

4. The thrower throws the ball direct into his own goal. What is the referee's decision?

No, because at the moment when A played the ball there were two opponents nearer to the goal-line.

....

Look at the diagrams carefully.

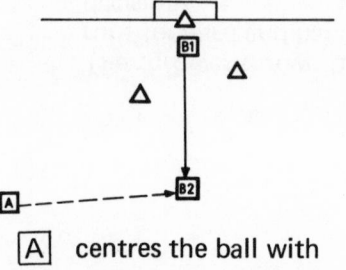 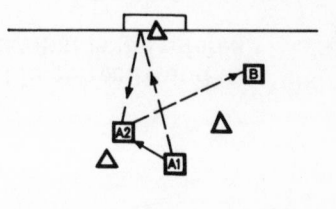

A centres the ball with B in position B1. B runs *back* to B2, collects the ball and scores. Is B off-side?

A shoots from position A1. The ball hits the crossbar and rebounds to A who has run to position A2. A passes to B who scores. Is B off-side?

_____

By a direct free-kick or a penalty.

....

Player A charges Player B fairly with his shoulder when Player B is waiting to receive a pass. The referee blows his whistle and awards an indirect free-kick. Why?

b. allow the penalty-kick to be taken first.

....

If the scores are level at the end of full-time and it is necessary under the rules of the competition for there to be a result with a winning side, extra-time may be played. The referee decides on the length of the interval between the end of the normal period of play and start of extra-time.

(Go straight on).

---

1. Direct free-kick.

2. Goal-kick.

3. Any of: throwing with one hand, not throwing from behind and over one's head, foot off the ground, foot in front of the line, not facing the field of play.

4. Corner.

....

THE GOAL-KICK AND CORNER-KICK

If the ball passes over the goal-line outside of the goal and was last played by one of the attacking side, there shall be a goal-kick.

If the ball was last played by one of the defending side, there shall be a corner-kick.

For a goal-kick or corner-kick to be awarded must the ball

a. be on the line?

b. wholly cross the outside of the line?

(Select the correct answer).

Yes.

....

Look at the diagram.

B1 shows where B was at the time that A passed the ball. B2 shows where B received the pass.

Is B off-side?

Give the reason for your answer.

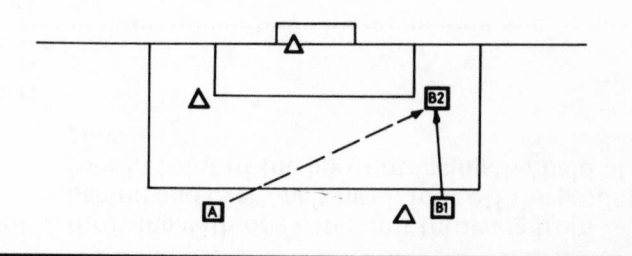

An indirect free-kick.

....

If a player charges fairly but the ball is not within playing distance of the player he charges, he will be penalized and an indirect free-kick awarded.

If a player charges in a violent manner, for example if he uses his elbow in an opponent's back, how should he be penalized?

THE REFEREE'S DISCRETIONARY POWERS OVER INFRINGEMENTS AND MISCONDUCT

When dealing with infringements and misconduct, the way in which the referee uses his powers is of great importance.

He should be firm and make his decisions quickly.

He should be completely fair and impartial in every decision.

He should penalize only deliberate breaches of the law.

Continual stopping of the game for trifling breaches of the rules angers the players and the spectators and spoils the match.

He should not penalize when to do so would give the advantage to the offending team. This is known as applying the advantage clause.

(Go straight on).

---

b. Wholly cross the outside of the line.

....

An attacking player kicks the ball towards the goal and a defender deflects it with his foot and it goes over the goal-line outside of the goal. Should the referee award a goal-kick or a corner?

B is off-side in diagram 2 because there are not two opponents between him and their own goal-line at the moment A plays the ball.

....

Look at the diagram.

A shoots for goal and the ball rebounds from the goal-post into play. B stops the ball and scores.

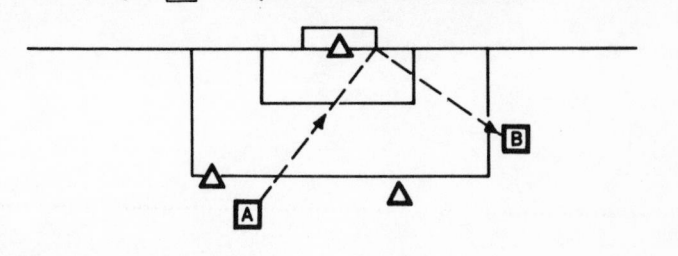

Is B off-side?

_____

b. an indirect free-kick.

....

The referee shall penalize a player who, he considers, is playing in a dangerous manner. The referee must judge whether a particular piece of play is dangerous and so liable to be penalized. Examples of play which could be considered dangerous are:

—kicking high at the ball when it is about to be headed by another player,
—kicking or trying to kick the ball when it is being held by the goalkeeper.

If he is penalizing a player for dangerous play, what should the referee award?

If, immediately after an infringment by a player of one team, the course of play favours the other team, the referee should not stop the game but should allow the advantage in favour of the team to continue.

For example, supposing that the centre-forward is tripped by the opposing centre-half but that he recovers at once and continues to develop an attack towards the opponent's goal, should the referee

a. award a free-kick?
b. apply the advantage clause and allow play to continue?

(Select the correct answer).

A corner.

....

A goal-kick is taken from the half of the GOAL-AREA nearest to the point where the ball crossed the goal-line. The ball is not in play until it has been kicked beyond the PENALTY-AREA. The opposing players should be outside the PENALTY-AREA while the kick is being taken.

Is the ball in play when it has travelled the distance of its own circumference?

He was in his own half of the field when the ball was last played.

....

Exception 2. *A player cannot be off-side if two or more of his opponents are nearer to their own goal line than he is.*

Both of these diagrams show the position of the players at the moment that the ball is played by [A] and the course that the ball will take.

In which diagram is [B] off-side?

Why is [B] off-side in one of the diagrams?

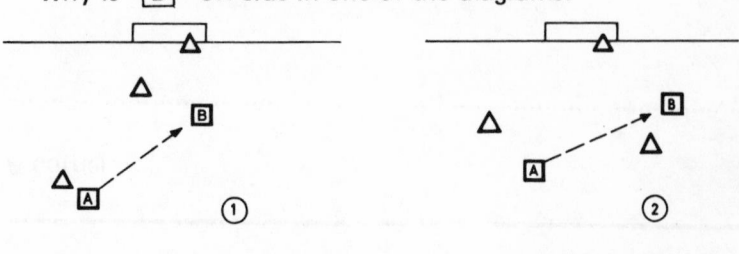

If a player commits any of the following five offences,

1. Playing in a manner considered by the referee to be dangerous.
2. Charging an opponent fairly but when he is not within playing distance of the ball.
3. Intentionally obstructing an opponent.
4. Charging the goalkeeper when he is not in possession of the ball in his goal-area.
5. If the goalkeeper 'carries the ball'.

the referee shall award

   a. a direct free-kick;
   b. an indirect free-kick.

(Select the correct answer).

b. allow play to continue.

....

The decision to apply the advantage clause must be taken immediately. Once he has decided to apply the advantage clause, the referee cannot change his decision.

A player of Team A holds the shirt of a player of Team B thus preventing him from reaching the ball passed to him. The ball rolls straight to another player of Team B who moves up field with it. Should the referee allow the advantage?

No.

....

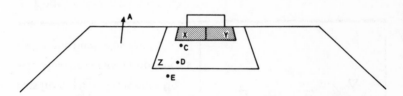

The ball crosses the goal-line at the point marked A.

1. Should the goal-kick be taken from the area marked X, Y or Z?

2. Is the ball in play when it has reached the point marked C, D or E?

3. While the kick is being taken the opposing players should be outside the

   a. goal-area,
   b. penalty-area.

Exception 1. *A player cannot be off-side if he was in his own half of the field when the ball was last played.*

Player [A] in position [A1] is in his own half of the field at the moment when [B] plays the ball. Player [A] is not off-side because he is in his own half of the field. Player [A] runs forward from [A1] to [A2] to receive the pass from [B]. He is not off-side when he enters his opponents' half of the field. Why not?

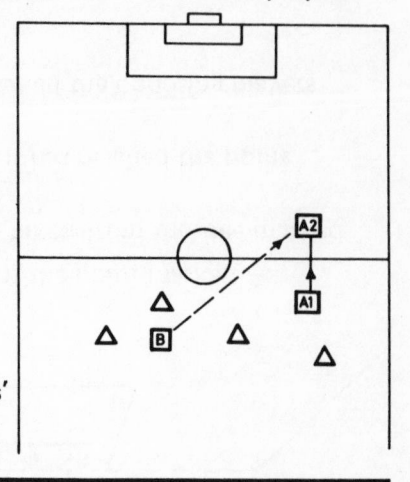

1. Foul or abusive language.
2. After the player has left the field.

OFFENCES FOR WHICH AN INDIRECT FREE-KICK IS AWARDED

An indirect free-kick is awarded if a player commits any of the following *five* offences.

1. Dangerous play.
2. Charging an opponent fairly but when the ball is not within playing distance of the opponent.
3. Intentionally obstructing an opponent.
4. Charging the goalkeeper when he is not in possession of the ball in his goal-area.
5. When the goalkeeper 'carries the ball'.

As you have learnt an indirect free-kick is also awarded for:

6. Off-side.
7. Persistently infringing the Laws of the Game.
8. Dissenting from the referee's decision.
9. Ungentlemanly conduct.
10. Kicking the ball again, after it has travelled its own circumference, and before it has been touched by another player after taking a corner, a throw-in, a direct, and indirect free-kick.

(Go straight on.)

Yes.

....

The Team B player, then, immediately loses the ball and Team A develops an attack. Can the the referee now change his mind and penalize the infringement?

_____

1. X

2. E.

3. *b.* penalty-area.

....

If the ball does not go beyond the penalty-area after a goal-kick, the kick shall be re-taken.

The kicker shall not touch the ball a second time before it has been touched by another player.

If the kicker touches the ball again inside the penalty-area, the kick is re-taken.

If the kicker touches the ball again outside the penalty-area, an indirect free-kick is awarded from the place where he touched it.

(Go straight on).

We have explained the basic off-side rule. There are four main exceptions. A player will be off-side if he is nearer his opponents' goal-line than the ball at the moment it is played, UNLESS

1. he is in his own half of the field;

2. there are two or more of his opponents nearer to their own goal-line than he is;

3. the ball last touched or was played by an opponent;

4. he receives the ball direct from a goal-kick, a corner-kick, a throw-in or when dropped by the referee.

We shall examine these exceptions now.

(Go straight on).

A player shouts abuse at the referee for awarding a penalty.

1. For what offence could the player be sent off?

2. If the player is sent off, when should the penalty be taken?

No, he cannot revoke his decision.

....

The referee has discretionary power to caution a player for *misconduct, ungentlemanly behaviour* or for *deliberately wasting time.*

When a player is cautioned, the referee must tell the player he is being cautioned, take his name, and send the name of the player cautioned to the Affiliated Association within two days (Sundays excluded). A referee who fails to report misconduct may be suspended if the misconduct is such that it should have been further investigated.

A player is cautioned on Saturday and the report on misconduct is sent the following Wednesday. Is this in order?

What should the referee do in these three examples.

1. The goalkeeper takes the goal-kick. He sees that the ball is not going to leave the penalty-area and so he runs forward and kicks it again before another touches it.

2. The goalkeeper mis-kicks the ball which goes sideways out of the penalty-area. He runs across and kicks it again.

3. The goalkeeper takes the kick but the ball stops inside the penalty-area. An attacker runs in and kicks it.

If he is nearer his opponents' goal-line than the ball at the moment when the ball is played.

....

However, a player who is in an off-side position should NOT ALWAYS BE PENALIZED.

A player who is in an off-side position should only be penalized if he is interfering with or influencing the game.

The referee, then, has these stages to his decision.

1. Is that player in an off-side position? Yes

2. Is he interfering with or influencing play?
   Yes   Penalize
   No   Don't Penalize

(Go straight on).

No.

....

A player shall be sent off for persisting in misconduct after a caution.

If a player is sent off and play is stopped in order to dismiss the player, a penalty-kick or a free-kick that is awarded shall not be taken until the player has left the field. The game is re-started by an indirect free-kick if no other breach of the law causing a penalty or a direct free-kick has been committed

(Go straight on).

No, the name should be sent within two days (Sunday excluded).

....

If a player is being cautioned, there are three things that the referee must do.
What are they?

1.

2.

3.

———————————————————————————

1. Have the kick re-taken.

2. Award an indirect free-kick.

3. Have the kick re-taken.

....

A goal cannot be scored direct from a goal-kick. However, a goal can be scored direct from a corner.
A player taking a corner-kick swerves the ball into the field of play and then straight into the net. What should the referee award?

b. the ball is played.

....

The basis of the off-side law is that a player is off-side if he is_____at the moment when the_____

---

1. For persistent infringements.

2. For dissenting from the referee.

3. For ungentlemanly conduct.

4. For entering the field after the start of play without the referee's consent.

....

OFFENCES FOR WHICH A PLAYER SHALL BE SENT OFF

There are three offences for which a player will be sent off the field. A player will be sent off

    1. if he is guilty of violent conduct or serious foul play;

    2. if he uses foul or abusive language;

    3. if he persists in misconduct after he has been cautioned.

Can a player, who has been sent off, return to the field later in the game?

1. Tell him he is being cautioned.

2. Take his name.

3. Report his name within two days.

....

The referee has the discretionary power to send a player off the field for the remainder of the game for violent conduct. He may also send off a player who has been cautioned but who persists in his misconduct. A player who has been sent off must also be reported within two days (Sundays excluded).

Can a referee allow a player, who has been sent off in the first half, to return after half-time?

_____

A goal.

....

A corner-kick is taken from inside the quarter-circle at the corner flagpost nearest to the point where the ball crossed the goal-line. The flag must not be moved. If the player, taking the corner, moves the flag, he must replace it before the kick is taken. A corner is awarded when the ball was last touched by

a. an attacker,
b. a defender before it crossed the line.

(Select the correct answer).

Yes.

....

This diagram shows the position at the moment that $\boxed{A}$ plays the ball.

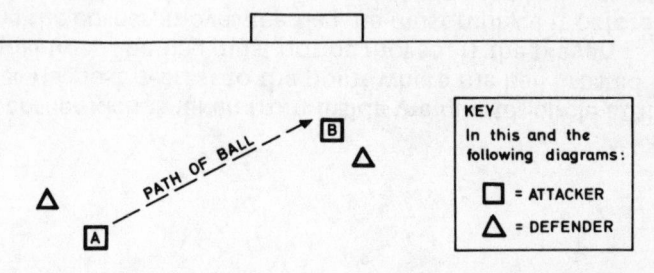

KEY
In this and the following diagrams:

$\square$ = ATTACKER

$\triangle$ = DEFENDER

Player $\boxed{B}$ is off-side because he is nearer his opponents' goal-line the moment that

a. he receives the ball.
b. the ball is played.

(Select the correct answer).

_____

1. Yes.

2. No.

....

When should a player be cautioned?

1.

2.

3.

4.

No.

....

The referee has the discretionary power to suspend or terminate the game if the weather makes it difficult to continue, or if there is serious disorder or interference by the spectators. He will only suspend the game after very careful consideration. After suspension he must fully report the matter to the Affiliated Association within two days (Sundays excluded).

If there is a long and heavy storm, should the players

a. run off the field to shelter?
b. await the referee's decision to suspend the game?

(Select the correct answer).

_____

b. a defender.

....

In order to get a better run up to the ball, the kicker removes the corner-flag and kicks the ball. What action should the referee take?

The basis of the off-side rule is that a player is off-side if he is *nearer his opponent's goal-line* than the ball at the moment the ball *is played.*

Note the two vital elements:

1. The player must be nearer his opponents' goal-line than the ball.

2. He must be nearer the goal-line than the ball at the moment *the ball is played,* and not at the moment that he plays it.

Is the deciding factor the position of the player in relation to the ball at the moment that it is played?

_____

No, it is re-started by dropping the ball.

....

A player has been off the field to have an injury attended to and wishes to re-enter the field. He must

   1. obtain a signal from the referee?

   2. wait till the ball is out of play until he can return?

b. await the referee's decision to suspend the game.

....

If the game has been suspended because of a storm, can the referee re-start the game when the storm has cleared?

Now turn to beginning of book page 63 (bottom).

Order the post to be replaced and the kick re-taken.

....

Players of the opposing team shall not be within 10 yards of the ball at a corner-kick until the kick has been taken. If they do so, the kick must be re-taken and the players ordered back from the ball. However, it may be to the attacking team's advantage to take a quick corner while players are still within 10 yards of the ball. In such a case, the referee will allow play to continue.

A corner-kick is taken and the ball is intercepted by a defender who was standing eight yards from the ball when the kick was taken. If there is no question of an advantage to the attacking team, what action should the referee take?

Now reverse book and turn to page 120 (top).

Section 4 Off-side

The off-side law is intended to prevent the attacking team from keeping players, close to the opponent's goal, waiting for the chance to score. Without the off-side law the attacker would have such an advantage that attacks would become uninteresting and lacking in tactical skill.

The development of attacks on the opponent's goal depends upon the correct understanding of the off-side law.

(Go straight on).

1. Persistent infringements.

2. Showing dissent from the referee's decision.

3. Ungentlemanly conduct.

If a player joins or rejoins his team after the match has started, he must receive a signal from the referee before he can enter the field of play. He need *not* wait until the ball is out of play. If he fails to get the referee's consent to join his team and he enters the field of play, the referee will stop the game, caution the player and re-start by dropping the ball where the offence occured. You have learnt that a player returning to the field after he has been sent to adjust his boots must wait for a stoppage of play and report to the referee.

If a player joins his team after the start of play without a signal from the referee. is the game re-started with an indirect free-kick?

POST-TEST ON SECTION 1

1. May a football field be square?

2. How many flags are essential to the field of play and what is the minimum permissible height of a flagpost?

3. What is the permissible weight and circumference of the ball?

4. What is the maximum permissible width of the lines marking the ground?

5. Will the goalkeeper be penalized if he handles the ball in the penalty-area?

6. Under what circumstances will substitutes for players be allowed in competitive matches?

7. If a player is sent off before the kick-off, may another player replace him?

8. Which of the following would be passed as satisfactory?

   a. Leather, screw-type studs with the screw as part of the stud and screwed into the boot.
   b. Rubber studs with metal plates covered with rubber.
   c. Combined bars and studs which are 1 inch in height.

9. A player has been sent off to adjust his boots.

   a. When may he return?
   b. Must he report to the referee?
   c. What action should the referee take if he returns at the wrong time?

Answers on page 62 (top).

1. *a.* Outside the penalty-area.
   b. At least 10 yards from the ball.

2. *a.* When it passed out of the penalty-area.
   b. When it has travelled the distance of its own circumference.

3. Indirect free-kick.

4. Indirect free-kick.

Now turn to Post-Test on Section 3 page 176 (top).

By an indirect free-kick.

Name three offences for which a player would be cautioned and the game re-started by an indirect free-kick.

ANSWERS TO POST-TEST ON SECTION 1

1. No.

2. Four, with a minimum height of five feet.

3. Weight = 14 to 16 ounces at the start of the game.
   Circumference = 27 to 28 inches.

4. Five inches.

5. No.

6. If the Rules of the Competition approved by the National or International Association permit.

7. Yes.

8. *a.* only.

9. *a.* During a stoppage.
   b. Yes.
   c. Stop the play and caution the offender.

Now turn back to page 41 (top) and continue with Section 2.

Indirect free-kick.

....

1. Where must the opposing players stand while

   a. a goal-kick is being taken?
   b. a corner is being taken?

2. When is the ball in play after

   a. a goal-kick?
   b. a corner?

3. What is the penalty if the kicker plays the ball a second time before it is touched by another player after a corner?

4. What is the penalty if the kicker touches the ball again outside the penalty-area after a goal-kick before it has been played by another player?

The referee must judge whether he considers a player to be guilty of ungentlemanly conduct. Behaviour which is normally penalized as ungentlemanly includes:
—a player deliberately wasting time;
—a player improperly calling out to an opponent;
—a player leaning on another player in order to gain height so that he can head the ball;
—a goalkeeper lying on the ball too long;
—players gesticulating and dancing about in an attempt to distract an opponent taking a free-kick or throw-in.

If the referee stops the game to administer a caution for ungentlemanly conduct, how would the game be re-started?

POST-TEST ON SECTION 2

1. Can a referee compel teams to change over at half-time without a break?

2. What are the two sets of circumstances for which a referee should add time to the end of a half?

3. When do a referee's discretionary powers begin?

4. The referee's discretionary powers allow him

   a. to_____ _____for any infringement of the laws;
   b. to_____a player for misconduct or ungentlemanly behaviour;
   c. to_____a player for violent conduct or persistent misconduct;
   d. to_____the game because of the weather or serious disorder.

5. Under what conditions can a referee change his decision?

6. What are the three things that a referee must do if he is cautioning a player?

7. If a player is seriously injured, what should a referee do?

8. What are the three main functions of a linesman?

Answers on page 119.

The corner-kick is taken and the ball hits the goal-post and rebounds to the kicker who then kicks the ball into the goal. What action must the referee take?

---

1. Yes.
2. A penalty-kick.

....

OFFENCES FOR WHICH A PLAYER SHALL BE CAUTIONED

There are four offences for which a player shall be cautioned. For three of these an indirect free-kick is awarded to the opposing side in addition to the caution being administered to the offender.

These three offences are committed.

1. when a player persistently infringes the Laws of the Game;

2. when he shows by word or deed that he dissents from a decision of the referee;

3. when he is guilty of ungentlemanly conduct.

(Go straight on).

ANSWERS TO POST-TEST ON SECTION 2

1. No, players have a right to a break at half-time.

2. *a.* For time lost through injury.
   b. For a penalty-kick to be taken.

3. When he enters the field of play.

4. *a.* stop play.
   b. caution.
   c. send off.
   d. suspend or terminate.

5. If play is not re-started.

6. *a.* Take his name.
   b. Tell him he is being cautioned.
   c. Report his name to the Affiliated Association within two days.

7. Stop the game at once and get the player to the touchline as soon as possible.

8. *a.* To indicate when the ball is out of play.
   b. To indicate which side is entitled to the throw-in, corner or goal-kick.
   c. To indicate that a player is in an off-side position.

Now turn back to page 74 (bottom) for Section 3.

Continued from page 117 (bottom).

Kick to be re-taken—defender ordered 10 yards from the ball.

....

The kicker must not play the ball a second time until it has been touched by another player. This is so even when the ball rebounds from the goal-post. If he does so, an indirect free-kick is awarded from the place where the infringement happened.

(Go straight on).

Continued from page 175 (top).

1. Kicking or trying to kick an opponent.

2. Tripping an opponent.

3. Jumping at an opponent.

4. Charging an opponent in a violent or a dangerous manner.

5. Charging an opponent from behind unless he is obstructing.

6. Pushing a player with hand or arm.

7. Holding a player with hand or arm.

8. Handling the ball.

9. Striking or trying to strike an opponent.

   a. Must these offences be intentional?
   b. If these offences are committed intentionally by a defender in his own penalty-area, when the ball is in play, what should the referee award?